Calm Up

Copyright © Sam Livermore, 2022

First Edition

ISBN (paperback) 978-1-914447-61-7

ISBN (ebook) 978-1-914447-62-4

Book Design by TGH International Ltd

Inner Illustatrions by Sam Livermore

Prepared by TGH International Ltd.

www.TGHBooks.com

Calm Up

Activate Your Calm

SAM LIVERMORE

DISCLAIMERS

Wherever you go,
There you are.

WHY CALM UP?

My genius is to help people create calm. Nobody likes to be told to calm down. It can feel patronising and also feels like our feelings don't matter and are being dismissed.

Rather than pushing down and suppressing our feelings which is what happens when we are told to calm down, **Calm Up** starts within, we go to the source of the feelings and discomfort in our body and start from there. This also happens when we use external sources to escape from the discomfort, we push down the feelings which can lead to overwhelm or not feeling anything at all.

Calm Up is not about negating or diluting what is going on in our life, it's about finding that place within all of us that is calm and using that to radiate out everywhere.

It's not about hitting a panic button as we can't cope anymore, it's about hitting an action button. The calmer we are the more present we are, and we can feel more connected to our relationships, our goals, and ourselves.

Calm is not just for other people, it's also for you, it's in all of us and you can access it too.

You can access your inner calm without sitting on a yoga mat for hours or being in constant meditation. You can feel more comfortable and at ease and have confidence in the choice you make. You don't need all the spiritual accessories, you just need more of you.

It's so easy to get overwhelmed with life and what is going on day to day, that we can forget to be present with our own feelings, we keep going through life's milestones, but knowing that something is not quite right. **Calm Up** helps you to connect to your own calm and create a sense of balance.

For years people have said that I am like human valium, that I exude calm, and if you have ever come to my #sharethelove stand at an event you may have even experienced it yourself. I hope I can bring you some of that calm as you read this book.

Start where you are.

We can only start at the beginning, right?

However, we sometimes compare our beginnings to other people's middles when it comes to self-development or business growth, or relationships.

We say to ourselves: *I should be further along than this.*

We look at others and say that's where I should be. But we haven't seen behind the scenes where they have been or how long they have been on that journey, what their trauma or privileges are. And unfortunately, nobody gets to skip the work. In other words, don't compare your apples to someone else's bananas. They look different and grow different.

So when you do any self-inventory throughout this book, you are the only person you are looking at and comparing yourself to.

I will be sharing personal stories alongside theoretical ideas and practical ways you can create your calm.

You will also find at the end of each section reflection prompts if you wish to journal on anything arising in your thoughts.

As you go through this book, you may choose to do any practical exercises or you may wish to carry on reading and come back to them later. If you are doing the reflection journal process as you read this may be enough, to begin with. You might not even want to journal the reflections if that's not how you process them. It may be enough to self-reflect in your mind.

Whatever works for you.

———

A BRIEF NOTE ON SYMBOLS

In 2016 I went to a workshop in London by Jennifer Hough, during the session we did a healing activation which was almost 30 minutes long. I was sitting in the front row with my friend and upon opening my eyes there were several symbols drawn on the flip chart. I gasped as I said to my friend oh my god, that's what I have been drawing for years. There were two symbols that I have been drawing since I was a small child. Jennifer asked who they belonged to as she had seen them bouncing around the room as holograms during the activation. I tentatively put my hand up as I said: "Two of them are mine I've been drawing them since I was little." She replied: "Well of course you have. They are healing codes and you are a healer." She went on to say there are 23 healing codes. I have been drawing 6 of them without even knowing what they are, I just found comfort in them. In between each chapter you will find one of these symbols that I have been drawing since I was around 4 years old. I was told off by teachers numerous times over my school years for defacing my books with them!

Sam Livermore

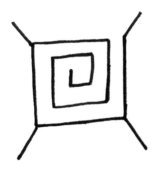

CHAPTER 1
WHAT DO YOU BELIEVE ABOUT YOURSELF?

hat do you believe about yourself?

Where do those beliefs come from? Do they come from something you have been told or something you have experienced?

Sometimes we have beliefs that come from a parent or family member's experience. We can inherit fears even though we have not had a bad experience with something. For example, you may have had a parent scared of cats and now you can't go near one, even though you have never had any contact with one to tell you they are scary.

Maybe you don't even know who you are deep down and have just followed the path given to you by your parents or caregivers, realising now that you are not as fulfilled as you expected to be.

What are some good things about you?

I ALWAYS FIND the answers interesting when I ask people this because they are often related to what we do for others. It is often easier to see ourselves in relation to others, but what about you as you?

What do you like about yourself as a being, not as a doing? This can be hard if you have never thought about this and the obvious thing to do is think of your physical self and focus on the things you don't like. But there will be things about your personality and your physical self that you appreciate but have felt like it's self-centered to focus on them. Maybe you have good humour and can make yourself laugh as well as others, or you have the ability to understand ideas quickly.

Do you know what you want?

IF YOU DON'T KNOW where you are going, it doesn't matter what road you take to get there.

Here's the thing, the place where you are going could be just across the road but if you don't know that, you could take a 30-mile round trip to get to it. I am reminded of the shepherd boy in Paulo Coelho's **The Alchemist**, who set out to follow his dreams and his journey took him on a long path to get to his destination, when he arrives he discovers he knew where his treasure was all along.

This is why we should have some clarity about what it is we want to set out to achieve. There may be times when on that road we take a little detour and it takes us away from our intention. Sometimes it may be a cul-de-sac and we have to make a u-turn. Other times it may be a shortcut that brings us out in front of traffic and then the annoying times when we think it's a shortcut but the road loops back around and brings us back to where we were!

In the past, I have felt like I have been in a maze of roads. I find the right turn then go merrily along the way, then suddenly decide to turn left only to find it's a dead end. However, if I had listened to my inner self I wouldn't have turned left in the first place. As I listened to my inner directions I got better at overriding the external directions that came from doubts and other people's ideas. Just like when a sat nav (or what you might call a GPS) tells you to turn left at the light and you know it's better to go straight on so you ignore it. It freaks out for a bit but then resets itself to the new route. If you have realised you have strayed off course, don't panic. Ask yourself, is this a direct path or am I trying to put up a roadblock or detour? Will this help or hinder my journey? Just reset your inner sat nav (GPS) and turn towards the direction you want to go.

I think this is why I trained in so many things because I wasn't actually sure what I wanted to do. I did not like school and my first job was in C&A, (a now-defunct department store) then a large toy store chain run by a giraffe, and then a large high street chain of chemists, well know in the UK. Not really having any qualifications on leaving school I could only work in retail. But after being out of work for nine years because of chronic illness and surgery, I had an opportunity to think about what I loved, which was psychology. I returned to college at 27, did a 1-year psychology course, then spent three years training as a psychodynamic counsellor. I had originally wanted to do criminology but the psychology teacher said I would be a great counsellor. One year after completing my training and working in a GP referral centre I realised I was living groundhog day and this was not what I wanted. I then moved into education and worked in 3 different schools over 14 years. On leaving education, I trained as a life coach (really only for the qualification for insurance) because of my counseling skills I passed with ease. I have since trained as an EFT practitioner, a crystal therapist, and a Reiki Master Teacher, with a few other modalities. Each time asking, is this what I want? And if unsure let's see what happens anyway.

Sometimes I criticized myself for changing my mind other times it has felt like the next step in the journey to here, gathering all the tools I have to create what I now do. I remember my dad saying to me once when I said I was going to do a particular training, *Oh so now you are going to be that, will that be the thing that makes money?* It made me feel like I was flaky and couldn't decide what to do or stick with one thing. I would tell myself I should just stay with one thing and spiral into self-doubt, but if it didn't bring me joy I just couldn't carry on.

You don't need other people's permission to thrive.

YOU CAN CHOOSE at every step of the way to make a change. Big or small it all adds up in the end.

And sometimes it can be a case of surrendering to the universe and seeing what comes next. That might not sound very calming, but we can get in our own way if we overthink things too much. We can get decision paralysis, wondering what other people will think, even people that don't know us that well. We often make decisions from our head, not our heart but is that always in our best interest? Who knows? It can go both ways, we can logic all we want but our heart can override it. Or our head can tell us how reckless we are being.

If you are stuck with a decision where all outcomes can be beneficial and they may just take you in different directions, but the decision means letting go of something longstanding it can be hard to take that leap.

I had a conversation with my nephew when he was around 20 and he asked my advice on something. He was wondering, *Will I have regret for not doing this?* I said to him it's better to have regret for doing something rather than not doing it because you can mark it up as experience rather than longing. The easiest thing to do is a pros and cons list. But commit to writing it in full truth, we can write these things down to make it go the way we want and ignore some of the pros or cons. It can be easy to write less on the con side to make the list look better if it's something we want to do and need to convince ourselves! To avoid this, write them on separate sheets of paper, and go all out on all your doubts and all your hopes. All the possibilities and realities. Leave it for a few hours or until the next day then come back to it with fresh eyes. It will bring you more clarity on making a decision from your own mind rather than someone telling you what to do.

That does not mean you never take advice, just that you don't follow other people's shoulds and learn to listen to your own guidance.

Reflections

Do my worries come from someone else?

*Do I know what I want or am I being
guided by someone else?*

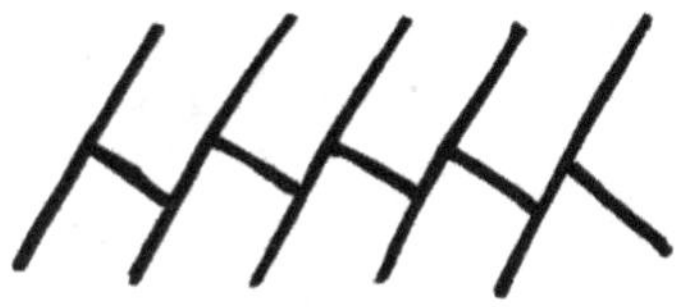

CHAPTER 2
IS IT A LIMITING BELIEF OR...?

We hear from so many places now about limiting beliefs. A lot of the time the phrase is not even used in context and over the last few years has become almost a gaslighting shameful way to tell someone it's just a limiting belief if you wanted to you could do it. Often in the context of someone trying to get you to join their program or sign up for high-priced coaching.

In psychological terms, a limiting belief is an emotional acceptance of some proposition, statement, or doctrine. This means that you have embedded on a deep psychological level that you are not able to do something, either because you think you are no good at it or because you as a person are not good enough. These often come from our teachers, parents, and other influential figures growing up. If we are always told we were rubbish at something even though we enjoyed it, eventually we either stop doing it or not put in any effort because there is the belief that we are not good enough so what's the point. How many of us say 'oh I'm rubbish at drawing' because we hold ourselves to the perfection of the school art teacher. Or 'I can't do maths' because of something that was said repeatedly in primary school.

Yes, sometimes it's a personal fear or pattern blocking us and sometimes it's the social structure we live in that is causing an actual barrier to doing a particular thing. Trying to build a business so you can leave a job, but while also doing that job you have caring responsibilities?

Not everyone has the support they need financially or emotionally, so you can mindset all you want but if you still need to work to pay rent and look after someone else then that's a physical barrier, not a limiting belief.

Have a physical disability and want to advance in your career? Is it a limiting belief that you can't get a promotion or is it societal conditioning that the average disabled person is not reliable or capable. When in my personal experience disabled people are the most adaptable and solution-focused people I know. Along with the actual physical spaces that are created by society meaning that not all workplaces are created equal.

**There is also the theory around
your thoughts creating your illness.**

Something that I once bought into 20 years ago but I cringe about now. While there is evidence that stress creates all sorts of impacts on our bodies which can lead to long-term conditions, saying that disabilities (or cancer or HIV) are because of some past life karma or unexpressed anger is not overcome by mindset, and just shames the person with a disability.

Nobody becomes an "overnight success" just by changing their mindset like some people would have you believe. Saying that we all have the same 24 hours in the day is another thing being said to shame people into thinking they are failing. If you are a carer, a parent, or disabled and don't have someone doing your shopping, cooking, cleaning, laundry, and admin then you literally don't have the same 24 hours as someone who has staff or support doing all of these things.

The above situations of external realities of society can't be changed by thinking more positively or pretending they don't exist. And I just want to scream when someone says just get up an hour earlier, or the most successful people get up at 5 am, NO just NO. These statements usually come from people with some sort of privilege or support that allows them to do this. Personally, I only get up at 5 am if I need to go to an airport. *Sleep is important*

The days of glorifying having 4 hours of sleep means you are succeeding in life are over. It hasn't escaped me either that most of these statements about getting up earlier are made by men or wealthy people, often not the ones dealing with children or the household tasks.

————

IT'S important when we are looking at our limiting beliefs to be clear on what is a deeply held belief and what is an external barrier that would need action to change. Sometimes an inner belief can be our perception (I can't draw because the teacher said so) or our reaction to the life situation we find ourselves in, that can come up when asked to draw at a meeting for example, when you're drawing is perfectly reasonable.

Sometimes it can be a reality, an external barrier physically stopping us from doing the thing we need to do, that can be solved by taking further action such as asking for help or support so you can achieve a goal. Other times it can be societal structures that we have little or no influence and being aware of that can make all the difference to our perception of a situation. I've lost count of the number of times I have done a business or personal interest training and the trainer has not understood the impact of fatigue, on the mind or body, implying that I didn't make enough time to do homework or preparation.

In today's society of on-demand access to so many things, can lead us to believe that we are not good enough if things don't work out for us straight away or we perceive that something should happen quicker because of what others tell us.

Ultimately I think we can only look at ourselves and what our beliefs are, not to be blamed for external circumstances and other people's attitudes. It's not just about positive thinking but being aware of our whole self, of how our thoughts and circumstances impact our whole physiology.

Sometimes you have to feel it to heal it

WHEN WE IGNORE the feelings telling us things are not ok, either they are causing fear, discomfort, or plain denial, we can use a number of things to pretend we are fine and to numb out those feelings.

Give yourself permission to feel.

SO OFTEN WE get a feeling that we don't like that tells us, *I don't like this situation*, and we immediately want to push it away. Instead of acknowledging to ourselves that this situation, person, or place is not ok for us, we do the most human thing of ignoring it by distraction.

We can block it out by numbing ourselves in all sorts of ways. We can use all sorts to stop ourselves from feeling, not just the obvious ways of alcohol and drugs to blot out our inner thoughts. It can easily lead to addictive behavior without even being aware of what is happening.

Perhaps we use exercise as a way to feel better, but it goes past the point of just getting fit and it becomes obsessive and unhealthy. Hours at the gym every day after work or running 20 miles a day when 10 miles will suffice. Going to the gym or yoga is more than your body can handle, but that feeling of exhaustion is covering up the feelings that we don't want to face up to. Shopping for things we don't need, buying clothes that never get worn. There is a high from buying them, but the only time they get worn is when they are tried on, and they just live in the wardrobe. This can often be followed by guilt and then a new shopping spree to get another high.

———

WHEN WE START to acknowledge all of our feelings, not just the happy ones, they leave quicker. So when you feel sadness, instead of trying to cover it up or pretend it's not there. Ask yourself these questions, *why am I sad?* You might surprise yourself. It may be as simple as I haven't seen my friend for a while and I feel a little lonely. I know that I am not eating well at the moment and this is affecting my mood. Or, it could be constant tiredness that has not even registered in your awareness because you are just on a day-to-day treadmill.

Am I honouring my moral standards?

Is there something going on that's not in line with my values and this is making me feel awkward?

The next question to ask yourself is,

Am I sad because of my own behaviour or someone else's? If it's someone else's, *is it something you have any control over?*

Are you able to have a dialogue with this person about what you would like to change? If there are too many things that come up here, choose 1 small action that could be implemented or worked on easily.

If it is something you have no control over and can't ask for or request change then it's time to look at whether that situation is still serving you. Is it possible to leave it? If not then it means coming to terms with the impact on your life. Of course, if that situation is causing you danger or severe emotional damage it's not possible to live with it as if nothing is happening, and confronting the person can make it worse, so it's about exiting in the safest possible way for you.

Sometimes when we feel like we have no control over the outside world it can show up as us controlling the smallest details in our life. We might start to control our food intake or how food is prepared and this can become obsessive. Or we start to structure our home routines very rigidly.

I remember when I was in a lot of pain in my twenties. I had a lot of books and videos (remember them?), they were organised in a very particular way on the shelves and I did not want anybody else to touch them.

If someone took one off a shelf without asking, I would be annoyed, maybe not even outwardly but inside I would be quite furious that they had messed up my system. Now I can tell you that 'my system' made no sense to anyone else.

You would assume that it was alphabetical or colour-coded or something normal like that, but no, because I was so desperate for some level of control over my environment, I had created a system that only I could know.

Books were organised by the order I had bought them, but also whether they had been read or not. So unread books were on a separate shelf but then after being read went next to the book that was bought before it. Videos were also in 2 sections, blank ones in the order I had recorded films and bought ones in the order of the most liked. It was also unbearable for me to see them not all perfectly flushed on the edge of the shelf, if one was slightly pushed in, I had to correct it. And yes this sounds absolutely bizarre, but this is what our mind can drive us to when we are looking for some element of control to feel calmer in our life. Looking back I realised I was actually creating control but not creating calm.

Now I'm a lot more relaxed about my books and have way less than I used to. I only have 1 particular category that has to be in order and it's entirely logical! My Paulo Coelho collection is in the order of publishing date. This makes sense because it's the whole collection alongside a signed card from him. And it doesn't matter if they are not all straight.

Often the only way out is through.

That first step of awareness is the most important. When we are aware we can do something about it. Or not. But we have the choice here, to take that first step towards feeling better about ourselves and feeling more in control. And when we feel more in control we can access our inner calm.

Reflections

---

*How often do I catch myself in a negative
thought loop?*

*Is there a way I can bring myself back to the
moment when I realise it?*

CHAPTER 3
HERE'S THE SCIENCE BIT

I would like to share what is going on in our brain on a chemical level so we can understand more about how our thoughts and reactions impact our levels of calm, both on a short and long-term basis.

When we have a positive thought about ourselves or someone else, or about the situation we are faced with, our brain releases a chemical called serotonin and this gives us the feeling of happiness and wellbeing. Serotonin acts as a conductor over the synaptic gap from brain cell to brain cell which allows for reflection, planning, and imagination. It enables us to create a train of thought.

When we have a negative thought about ourselves or a situation we are faced with, the brain releases a chemical called cortisol. This is not bad, it's part of our fight or flight response, however, when we are in a fear response the pre-frontal cortex in our brain that allows a train of thought is hijacked, and that's why we often do irrational things when we are angry or in fear. We also block the part of our brain that allows for reflection so we only see more of the problem and not the solution. When we are in a stress response, our heart rhythm increases or is erratic, around 1400 biochemical changes are happening in our body, this directly affects our performance, the incoherence inhibits our brain function and our organisation is impaired as we think less creatively.

We literally can't see the wood for the trees.

EVER BEEN LATE for an important appointment because something has happened in the morning while getting ready or you have got bad news?

Then it seems like everything is going wrong, you can't find your keys even though they are always in the same place, the stress makes us blind to them. You might notice in this situation your breathing is shallow or you feel like you have a headache starting, that is the cortisol surging through your system as your brain focuses on more of the problem.

In small amounts, cortisol has anti-inflammatory properties; it is released during sleep and can stay in your system for up to 13 hours. There are only two things that can help metabolise cortisol, relaxation, and exercise. Over time a build-up of cortisol in our system can metabolise to cortisone if your body produces too much of it. Cortisone is found in high levels in people with anxiety and depression. Studies have also found that it can lead to diabetes and reduces calcium absorption. I also discovered when researching auto-immune diseases that cortisone is often high in that group too. It's the accumulative build-up over time of the stress response that causes harm to the body.

———

BY THINKING POSITIVELY, we release serotonin which makes us feel happy, and when we feel happy we open up our brain to new thought connections. We see more of what's right about a situation rather than what could go wrong. It's why when we are in a stress response, taking a moment to take slow deep breaths in for 5 and out for 5, actually brings us back into focus. It puts our brain into competency mode, which allows us to reflect and be clearer in our planning.

Sometimes it's easy to go on a train of memories just from one little thought, reliving whole moments of relationships or situations hearing other people's words in our minds when trying to focus on one thing. Our brain can take us back to a particular time through an overheard comment, a song, or a smell. Our senses will refire those synapses all in milliseconds and before you know it you are reliving some scenario.

How do you bring yourself back to the moment and the task at hand when that happens to you? Especially if it takes you on a spiral of unpleasant memories? When I catch myself in an unpleasant thought loop, I say BE HERE NOW and ask to cancel, clear, and delete that thought. I take a deep breath hold it for a moment and then breathe out slowly. That brings me back to focus on where I am.

The only thing that can clinically lower the stress response is relaxation and exercise.

So make sure you are taking that time to meditate (whatever that means to you) this could be moving meditation, walking, or cycling not just sitting in traditional meditation. Eat well for your immune system, as much fresh food as you can including vitamin C, Zinc, Vitamin D, and the B vitamins, all have a role in helping your nervous system function well. Do some form of exercise (whatever you enjoy) to ensure you are managing your cortisol levels.

Stressors are external causes that create a reaction, according to our perception of an event. Everyone is different in their reaction and even their perception of stressors, which is why people can sometimes look confused at others' reactions to a situation that they don't find stressful at all. Stress management is not about taking away the stress, it is about helping you manage your reaction so you can have more control over your emotions and physical response.

We also have a natural body response to shock and pain which you have probably forgotten about because as children we were told to stop doing it, so you have developed a response that it is wrong so your brain has trained your body not to do it. Do you remember as a child if you fell over or had a shock, your body would shake? That is a natural response to trauma. It is your body processing and moving the trauma through your body. Have you ever seen a nature documentary where a lion is chasing a group of gazelles and as he picks one off the others will run and then lie down? You might see them laying still and then start shaking. They then stand up and carry on with their business. The tremor is the body's way to move trauma through us.

But as children we were told to stop shaking, you're ok, don't worry there is nothing going to hurt you, stop shaking. So we think it's a bad thing to do.

———

I REMEMBER some years ago when my body was in a serious disease flare and I had to go to an appointment, when I got home I fell in the chair and couldn't move for an hour. I was so tired. As I tried to get up to lay on the bed, I was in so much pain and barely able to move. As I tried to shuffle across the room my body started shaking violently. I could barely breathe, I made it to the arm of the sofa and fell on it, with my body shaking so much I had to hold onto the wall. After the initial panic, I realised what was happening and began to breathe into the shaking and could feel it move through me from top to bottom. I sat like this for 10 minutes until the shaking stopped naturally and when I stood up to go to the bedroom I was surprised at the ease I now felt in my body. My brain and body had worked together to process the shock of the pain so it was a little easier to move than before.

Now we have a basic understanding of how our brain helps and hinders us we can go deeper into activating our own calm.

Reflections

What feeling do you find yourself avoiding?

*Have you noticed something you do to
avoid this feeling?*

CHAPTER 4
IS YOUR TABLE OFF BALANCE?

Our mental, physical, emotional, and spiritual bodies can be affected by our beliefs either one or all of them. We can often know something intellectually but not believe it on an emotional level.

I imagine it as a table. If one leg is shorter than another, it will be off-balance and you might be able to prop it up temporarily so it doesn't wobble. You know you need to do something but haven't got the time so you make do. But if two legs are different lengths from the others you start to notice how annoying it is. You might consider, well I can fix this one easily but the other one will just have to stay propped up. What if you get all four legs at different lengths? It's an unusable table and we would rather not use it. So instead of acknowledging the broken table, it gets ignored, left in a corner and we pretend that it's fine. We use other things instead of the table to cover up the fact the table is broken. Or in extreme scenarios, we prop up every leg to make a very wobbly table rather than looking at how to fix it. We are in denial that there is something wrong with the table, even though other people notice how wobbly it is. You might not even be aware that your table is wobbly as you have been using it for so long.

This sounds like a mammoth task to fix your table, or even just make it nicer to use so I'm going to share some easy tools that are often overlooked or seen as something that doesn't work. This might not fix your table all in one go, but it will help you become aware of how out of balance it is. All you need to do first is take the first step towards change and that is awareness.

Affirmations

BEFORE YOU ROLL your eyes and say *"oh I've tried that and it doesn't work"* or *"I'm not into the Law of Attraction"* Let me give you a different take on how to phrase your affirmations so your mind doesn't respond with the thoughts of this *isn't true, this is ridiculous, and you don't really believe this.* If you don't really feel it on the inside or know what it's like to experience that feeling or situation your mind will reject affirmations.

So how about phrasing it as a question instead? When we ask ourselves a question, the brain will search for an answer, it will start to look for ways this could be possible. It will start to see possibilities of ways this could happen that you might have not noticed. In the same way that you decide you are going to buy a particular model of car in the colour blue, your mind will start to make you notice them in places you didn't before. You will see them pass you on the street, in ads, in car parks, it's quite magnificent how the brain works.

Instead of saying, I am calm and centered when you are really panicking, say what would it be like to feel calm right now? In what ways can I feel calm right now. What feeling would I be having if I was calm right now? As you move into that feeling, the physiology of your body changes and the brain is searching for ways to bring you answers instead of arguing back to you by saying: "But I don't feel like that." Just that small shift in our mental and emotional state can give us more balance than we realise.

Emotional Freedom Technique (EFT) or Tapping

EMOTIONAL FREEDOM TECHNIQUE is a tool that can be used for many things, it's a simple process where you tap lightly on different points on your face and upper body that align with meridian points, think of it like acupuncture, but instead of needles, you tap on points instead. While tapping you say what you are feeling, whether it's physical symptoms or emotions. (see resources section)

I first used EFT for pain relief after it was recommended to me, and I followed a few online videos. It was bizarre to me how it worked and when I looked for training opportunities to learn more about it, I found one coming up a few weeks later by a master trainer that had been in the first 10 people to train in it in the UK, in a location 30 minutes away, what were the chances! This was 2014 so not as many as there are now, after doing the introduction and finding out how it works on a deep level of your stored emotions, I went on to train as a practitioner a year later. I feel blessed that I was trained in pure EFT by someone who had been trained by Gary Craig, the person who popularised it as an energy healing tool.

I have noticed in a whole section of the self-development community there is a thing about not being negative, or saying negative things, only thinking and saying happy thoughts. If we keep repeating the same complaints over and over and not taking action or helping to change them, that's one thing, but expressing your feelings to process them is a good thing. I often say we need to feel it to heal it. That's why EFT is good for moving those negative emotions through the body. Saying what is bothering us while tapping on the meridian points can shift the energy disruption through our bodies. It's a quick in-the-moment tool. You can even say it in your mind when in public and tap on your hand and fingers. (I have free EFT resources on my website)

Standing in our power.

CHANGING your body stance can bring a quick change in your emotional state and other people's perceptions of you. And when other people's perception changes it mirrors back to ourselves, therefore, increasing our own positive self-perception.

We can do this by changing our posture, whether sitting or standing. Holding our head up, looking forwards instead of down, unclenching our hands, breathing into our belly, not our upper chest. All of these will change our physiological state and have an effect on our own bodies.

There is no such thing as multi-tasking

WE DO NOT MULTI-TASK, we multi-focus. When we are trying to do several tasks at once we are not giving all the attention to each task, our attention is split across them. So each time we change tasks we change focus, giving more focus to the one at hand and less to the one we were just doing. As much as we think we are multitasking we are not giving each task the full attention it deserves or needs. It's why we can leave a room to do something in the middle of one task and get fully into another, only remembering where we were at when we return to the room. We have moved to a different place out of view of the original task so our focus is shifted.

It's said that women are better at multi-tasking, or are they just having to multi-focus out of necessity because of the many responsibilities of children/home/work? When we are splitting our focus over too many things at once for extended amounts of time it can cause brain fog. Every time we change to focus our brain has to reassess the task at hand and the surrounding environment. It needs to know how much attention to pay.

Have you ever wondered why you sometimes need silence to see better? It's so you can focus your full attention on what you are looking at without your brain doing auditory processing in the background.

Hence we turn down the radio in the car when driving in a new area as we need to find the place we are looking for. Or we tell people to be quiet so we can focus on the route if it suddenly changes.

Focus on one task at a time, give it your full attention, and it will get done quicker than if you are trying to do several things at once.

Reflections

Where might I be off-balance?

*Which one of these can I use next
time I feel like this?*

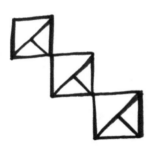

CHAPTER 5
IS THIS IT?

D o you know the Jim Rohn quote: *You are the average of the 5 people you spend the most time with.* That's all very well in an ideal scenario but I think it's also quite guilt-making too if you are trying your best. What if you don't have a lot of friends, what if you are the main carer for someone or you are a single parent and trying to hold down a business too.

When I first heard this some years ago, I thought well that would be my parents then and a couple of friends that to be honest were not the most inspirational. It made me feel like I was not the person I was, it made me question my inner values that were quite different from my parents. It gets shared a lot in personal development circles, and I think we need to consider that it's not as empowering as we think it is.

How about when we hear this we think well the 5

people I'm with most of the time have these values and gifts for me, but if I want to be better or grow in my life and these people cant support me with that then what do I do?

I started to think okay: Who *would I have at my imaginary table of 5?*

When our external circumstances don't fit the so-called ideal of some of the self-development stuff out there, we can adapt it to our own needs. I like to think of it as a platter, I'll have a bit of that but that part doesn't taste nice so I'll leave it thanks.

With my table of 5, there are not always the same people because hello they are my imaginary friends, I listened to their podcasts, read their content, and looked at how I could be supported by what they offered until I started to internalise it and offer myself that support. And it sounds so trite and annoying to hear, but when you change on the inside the outer changes too, and you attract the people that support you at the level you are. It might only be in the virtual space in some situations but it really does happen.

This is why I think that when you work on yourself things can change because the universe, God, spirit, whatever you want to call it, supports change. It's the only constant we have. We like to blame things on others and things outside of our control, that's what human beings do, but the only thing you can control is yourself and your reactions.

.   .   .

WHEN I WAS A TEENAGER, I went to a youth club from the age of 14 (oh the 80's when stuff like that got funded) and I met my friend, Joe, with who I'm still friends today. Joe has spina bifida and is a few years older than me, he used the youth club so he could extra practice shooting hoops. I was mesmerized by him every week in a wheelchair with a basketball. After a few months, he said to me: *I play in a team and we have a game this weekend if you want to come to watch.* So I got a bus to this sports centre and it blew my mind. Being an odd teenager and not having a lot of friends I got involved with volunteering, a year later I found myself at the wheelchair games at Stoke Mandeville. I actually took a week off school to do this. It was the best time of my young life, I didn't feel like the odd one or awkward I finally felt like I fit in. No one noticed my hidden disability which people at school made fun of. And I discovered so many sports I had no idea was happening. But then I had another issue, I can't tell people at school as they will think I'm even weirder and I'll have even fewer friends! I actually got fully involved in wheelchair basketball when I left school and even ran a team for a year when I was 19, not quite sure how that happened I'm sure it was Joe's fault. Haha!

Eventually, I had to give it up being at work and

managing my own health I couldn't do it all. It was like giving up a whole identity. Who was I without this group of people? Of course, some friendships endured outside of the sport, and I still went to the occasional game with Joe. *But it was like I had to fit in all over again.*

Have you ever felt like that?

YOU BECOME SO INVOLVED in something because you don't like who you are inside, you find that place that gives you the confidence to be who you are when you are with them, but when that ends eventually you have to come back to yourself.

My Grandad used to say *'wherever you go, there you are'* I didn't get it at the time, but now whenever I feel like I want to escape, I ask myself what am I escaping from? Is it me or do I actually just need a change of scenery? And then I address whatever it is that needs to come out. It's much better to go through the feelings about a situation than go around it or try to get away, it will always be there until you actually meet it head-on.

And what about my love of what is now the Paralympics widely loved by so many? London 2012 was so emotional for me, talking to strangers on the tube on the way, seeing everyone in the Olympic Park, and feeling the buzz of excitement from everyone. I cried at seeing so many people realise the power of disability sport. That teenage part of me felt at peace and no longer weird, I felt sort of special in a way like I had known a secret that others had just found out.

When I think about who I am today compared to who I was 10 years ago, I can see how different I am. Of course, we change, we grow and we are affected by external situations that we live through (hello 2020) but also I can see how I was not expressing my full self because of the job I was doing at the time.

But then I look back even further and can see whenever I listened to the whispers of my heart, expressed myself, and was able to say what I believed in, being open about spiritual practice my health and wellbeing was inflow. When I have been in jobs, mostly education, I have had to hide that witchy, mystical part of myself it has either affected my physical wellbeing or my mental health.

Trying to pretend you are not that weird is exhausting! It's easy to lose yourself to try and fit in with what society deems acceptable. If you are in a battle with yourself every day over who you need to be you will eventually question what you are even doing.

Have you ever asked yourself the question: *what is it all about"* or *"is this it?*

That's when you know you have lost yourself. Sometimes it can take us time to get to this question as we don't want to hear it. When you get to the point that you can no longer sustain this feeling and you know you need change, it will be very clear to you.

I remember walking into work one day in 2013 and feeling like I had waded into treacle. Just in that moment as I walked up the school corridor I felt the shift and knew that I could no longer do this. As much as I loved the kids that I worked with and my actual work I could no longer deal with the environment. I had been feeling like that for a while and was focusing a lot on my self-development and noticing how dysfunctional the relationships were at work. Even though I had trained as a counsellor years before, it was when I reconnected with myself that I saw the patterns being mirrored to me were not making me happy. Later that day, I had a moment where I literally could not breathe, just suddenly it struck me standing there in the school office, I sat down and was gasping for air, they ended up calling an ambulance, who took me into hospital just in case because of my medical history. Three months later, I had given in my notice and left. I just couldn't sustain being in that environment anymore.

Look at your relationships, with people, places, and things. Are they evolving or dissolving? There is only one constant and that is change, we are always going in one direction or the other nothing stands still if it's standing still then it is not alive.

Reflections

Where am I resisting change?

Who would I be without....
(this thing, person or place)?

CHAPTER 6
USE THE POWER OF YOUR WORDS WISELY

Do you have a moment in your life that you go back to in your mind, and say 'I wish I'd never said that, or did that' ...? Even if it was a long time ago and you may have apologised or you have moved on from that situation?

I have a moment from my 20s that is replayed in my mind sometimes, even though I understand why I did it and even talked about it with this person years later and apologised. I think it echoes sometimes when I'm in a dynamic with someone who is sarcastic or unapologetic for their actions and takes no self-responsibility. I see myself from that moment years ago.

At the time I was in a lot of physical pain and used sarcasm a lot to negate the pain I was in, and it sometimes landed on the closest people around me.

This particular friend I had known since I was 16 and we were close.   Sadly they passed away in 2019 at the early age of 53.   I remember just saying a throw-away comment which I thought was funny, them going into the bedroom, not coming out, and then I left.   Have you had something like that happen to you?

It took a few weeks for us to be back on proper terms again, and we talked about it in our 30s, when we were both a lot more emotionally mature having been through lots of personal growth in relationships and come out of the other side. But when do we translate our inner learning to how we relate to others in real life? What if that person doesn't want to forgive, move on, or grow from the experience? What if you can't move on and are stuck in time.

As they say: 'you can lead a horse to water but you can't make them drink.

That's when you have to stop and assess, am I living and growing or am I just surviving. I've certainly been through times like that in my life, in different situations regarding my work and relationships. I realised that when we don't face our pain then we can't get to our peace.

We can create anxiety in ourselves when we have a different persona in public to the one we have with close friends or family, or even ourselves. I'm not talking about the difference between being professional for work and more relaxed with friends, but being a chameleon and creating a persona that we know doesn't align with our true self, but it feels necessary to be liked. Those things can take a toll on our mental health because it feels like putting on an act.

First, find peace within yourself then you can also bring it to others – Thomas A Kempis

circa 15c

I read this quote sometime in my mid-30s and it was a light bulb moment. I wrote it down on a post-it note that I still have. When we face our pain, our darkest thoughts, and our regrets, it leads us to a resolution inside ourselves, even if we can't get a resolution with others. When you feel peaceful you can react with peace.

Remember that rhyme when you were young, "sticks and stones may break my bones but words can never hurt me"? That never really sat well with me even as a child, words do hurt, they can have a massive effect on your daily life. Words are so powerful. Think of that feeling you get when someone says they love you. You feel it right in the centre of your being, it vibrates through your heart you feel a sense of wonder. Now think of the times when someone has said something hateful. It has the same power. You feel it in your stomach. It still vibrates through your whole being...just like love does.

———

HAVE you seen the research by Dr. Masaru Emoto and water crystals? It is really amazing. He has shown through science the power of words on water crystals. As our bodies are around 70% water this has amazing implications on how our body is affected by the words we hear every day. In his short video 'Water, Consciousness and Intent' you can see images of water crystals and how they were affected by words and music.

We need to be so mindful of the words we are using, and how we talk to ourselves and each other. We also need to be mindful of who else is hearing our words even if they are not the recipient. After working with children for many years, it is surprising how many parents don't realise the effect on their children overhearing arguments and discussions. Even when they are not in the same room the power of negative words vibrates intensely they can still be absorbed by others in the range of the sound.

Use the power of your words wisely, I remember my Grandma used to say "if you don't have anything nice to say, don't say anything at all".

When you are about to criticise or be negative about something think WAIT, Why Am I Talking. Do you need to express this negativity, will it be helpful or will it exaggerate the situation? Uninvited advice can be received as judgment, unless you have context on a situation or someone asks it's always best to keep it to ourselves.

It can be scary to admit we have these inner thoughts, even to admit to ourselves is hard let alone share them with another person. It can be hard to look at how our past behaviour towards others, when we have been in despair, which has then caused upset for them and yourself. In a 12-step program commonly used for addictions, they call this making amends. This can be a very effective way of processing your thoughts around past actions and events. Perhaps you remember a time when you engaged in gossip or superficial chat that you thought was normal at that time, it's how people related to each other but it didn't feel good.

Write out anything from your past that is still on a thought loop where you wished you had acted differently. Write about what happened from your perspective at that time, as you are writing you may have a realisation of

'I acted like this because at the time I felt...'

This exercise can help you let go of the thought loop, you may remember parts of the situation that your mind had blanked out, and you may no longer have that person in your life and have been holding on to it because of guilt, shame or even anger.

If you feel guilty about the way you acted towards someone you may want to write them an apology letter afterward, you don't even need to send it will still work on an energetic level.

This is where the Hawaiian prayer Ho'pono'pono can be very helpful.

I'm sorry

Please Forgive Me

Thank you

I Love You

You can say this prayer while holding that person or situation in your mind, just repeating it for 1 minute will send out ripples of forgiveness to you and the other person or people involved. If you want to learn more about the Ho'pono'pono I recommend the book *At Zero* by Joe Vitale.

Sometimes we can be holding onto this thought loop because we felt we were wronged by another person and are still feeling angry about it. Angry at them or angry at ourselves for not reacting in a particular way. I love the words of the Buddha that says, holding onto anger is like holding a hot coal and expecting the other person to get burnt. This anger can be justified of course but holding on to it years later helps no one.

This is where forgiveness can be powerful, forgiving does not mean you condone the behaviour of that person. You forgive for your own peace, not for the other person. If you have not been able to tell that person how you feel and are still holding onto what you wanted to say or would say if you had the chance, then now is the time to let their words go onto paper, write the ho'pono'pono at the end, for yourself and the person you were at the time. By using the ho'pono'pono in this situation you can release any anger towards yourself. I would then suggest ripping up this letter and disposing of it or burning it safely. (hint: don't burn things indoors!)

Reflections

---

*Is there a past situation that
I'm holding onto?*

Is it time to let it go?

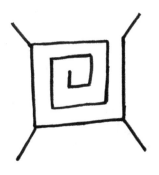

CHAPTER 7
WHAT DOES IT FEEL LIKE TO SAY NO?

Do you remember when you were young thinking about how you would change the world? But then as you get older you start to realise that it's not actually that simple.

I'm sure you've heard that story of the boy throwing starfish back into the sea and when a man says it's pointless they will just come back again, and the boy says that's ok if I can save just one I have made a difference. That's where we start with changing the world, we look at the small actions from ourselves.

I used to get so overwhelmed with how to tackle the homeless problem we have and think about what a huge thing it is to overcome and then I realised if I make a difference to one person then it's still a change to that one life. I don't have to solve the whole thing. Yes, I still struggle when I see multiple homeless people on the street, I can't help them all and sometimes I feel guilty if I buy someone a cup of tea and am not able to do it for everyone that is there. But I know that I make a difference to that 1 person. Sometimes it's easy to think why even bother, what is the point when it's the system that needs changing?

Where do you do that in your life? Where do you hold back from making that small change in your life because you think what is the point, it won't change anything. Here is the thing though, all those little changes accumulate into something bigger. Whether it's for you or someone else, it's the small things that matter, sounds cheesy but it's true. When you look at the bigger picture you never know how your small action impacts another, and then they impact another and it goes on and on through the day.

Imagine you are in the supermarket, and someone bumps into you, how do you react? Do you brush it off and carry on or do you lash out and carry that resentment around the whole shop.

How does this impact the rest of your day, and theirs too? I'm not saying you have to turn into a saint and be forever thinking about not doing or saying anything to upset another person, that's impossible we are human. But if you start to look at interactions with a sliding doors perception it makes life more interesting.

If you have not seen the 1998 film Sliding Doors, it popularised the term sliding door moments. These are seemingly inconsequential small moments that can go on to have a huge impact on relationships in our lives, like the butterfly effect. When I was 9 we moved house because of a constantly leaking roof, actually just across the street from where we were. I often think if we had moved to the house they first showed us 1 mile away would I have gone to the youth club or got involved in disability sport?

Unlikely, or maybe not?

When we examine our interactions and relationships with others, even the transient ones, we can see how all things are connected. It's sometimes called the Kevin Bacon effect, or more formally 6 degrees of separation we can all connect ourselves to another person on the planet in just 6 connections.

If you are an introvert or people pleaser you have probably gone through a big chunk of your life doing things for others on autopilot, and as you have you dived into your self-development and learnings over the years realised that some of those people have an expectation of who you are.

You may become aware that they don't share any words of gratitude or in some situations a request for your help because they just assume that's how it is. And the longer it goes on in your awareness the more you realise the power of those few words that are missing. Especially if words of affirmation is your love language.

———

I DON'T KNOW about you but I've had a struggle in the past with feeling some guilt around wanting to be thanked. An internal monologue that goes,

"but they are my friend of course I would do that, but they didn't ask me they just expected it, I might have offered them anyway, but they just assumed without checking with me, but they are my friend I shouldn't feel like this"

and round and round it goes.

This is even harder if your main love language is quality time (which mine is) because you want to spend that time with them but feel taken advantage of.

You might even be thinking but do I say the things I want to hear enough to others after all the world is a mirror and are we giving what we want to receive? If the answer is yes I do then that can be a hard thing to swallow.

What does it feel like to say no?

I mean not for things that we know will put us in danger, like no I will not drive recklessly or do something illegal but when we have to stand up for ourselves when it crosses our personal or moral boundaries.

When I was younger I would easily go along with things just so I didn't rock the boat even if I didn't particularly want to do something, I was called 'easy going' but on the inside sometimes there was resentment. And then when I did disagree or say no I don't want to do that I was called selfish.

It's interesting isn't it, we can be seen as easygoing and open to persuasion but when we actually do stand our ground or be courageous enough to enforce boundaries then we are told we are the opposite.

And if you are someone that grew up with conflict or witnessing intimidation it's easy to not want to rock the boat so when you are called selfish you back down and agree, therefore building even more resentment.

You could say that growing up in that environment leads you into those sorts of relationships or that maybe you had to pretend to be nice a lot as a child to get access to school friendships and you don't know how to have a give and take relationship.

I think I used to be somewhere in the middle, I wasn't allowed to have school friends in my house growing up, and I never had a birthday party or friends around for dinner. I had to make excuses all the time to my friends. So I would agree to doing whatever they wanted to be able to hang out with them.

Over the last 15 years or so, (after personal therapy and a lot of healing from my childhood) I started to say no to friends when they encroached on my boundaries or took energy from me that I would need days to recover from. I had pushback from those people and it made me realise how a lot of them were not equal friendships, I was doing a lot of giving and not much receiving (mostly because they did not give)

I had the courage to step away from those people, it's not easy, especially when you realise how manipulated you have been.

So I want to say to you, it's ok, you have permission to feel good about it, to know that you are stepping into more of who you are when you let go of people that don't have your best interests at heart. And when you know what you cherish in yourself and others you will deepen the connection with the friends and family that have rode the wave with you.

When you start to give to yourself and put your needs first, you will see how it is not selfish it is self-full. And that's not in a negative way. How many times have you heard someone say, oh they are so full of themselves, and it's said as a criticism? Maybe you have even said it yourself. I think that comes from a place of not feeling good enough about ourselves and we see that this person has high self-regard, in other words, yes they put their needs first. But it can be done in a way where you are kind and respectful to others, being self-full does not mean you have to be rude when saying no.

———

So how do we receive those words that we want to hear?

Boundaries

Saying no when you would normally say yes because it's expected of you, and you really want to say no. Saying that won't work for me when someone just expects you to do the thing that would actually encroach on your time and your needs.

You might not hear those words from those people that you set boundaries with, but the universe will deliver them from elsewhere too. As you step more into your needs and your boundaries other people around you will see a shift, they are more likely to gravitate towards you, while the person that rode roughshod over your boundaries can't actually believe your audacity.

I noticed that it goes across all areas of your life, say a regular no to someone in your friend group and at work, your boundaries become clearer, without even saying anything. And vice versa. As a result, your self-care goes up, you start saying those words more to yourself and meaning them. You feel calmer and more centred and every interaction is easier.

Reflections

---

*What words do you need to
hear more of?*

*Where do you say yes when you
want to say no?*

CHAPTER 8
THE BODY REMEMBERS WHAT THE MIND FORGETS

We can often be hazy around past events in the mind but the body will easily slip into the fear response when confronted with cellular memory. It's what happens with phobias, we often don't even know why we are scared of something irrational, but it often goes back to a bodily memory from early childhood. Our body can alert us to things that we may not even have a physical memory of because it's too painful, but certain situations can make our body think it is happening again. It can make us look like we are overreacting to some people but it can be very visceral and in the moment for us.

Years ago I worked with someone scared of banana skins, we thought it was quite odd and funny, but it was very real to her. When I later trained in psychology and counselling I realised that her fear had most likely come from a traumatic event as a child where there were banana skins present and she wouldn't have even realised. Her body fixated on a small detail while her mind was processing the event.

This is also why when we replay memories, good or bad, we can access the same body memories. Your body does not know the difference between you remembering something from years ago or the other day, it will go straight back to that time. Your body can even hold ancestral memories passed down from your parents and grandparents.

As I mentioned earlier on about the body shaking to process shock, we can encourage our body to release any held on to tension through an exercise similar to the natural tremor response. Lay flat and gently move your hips or pelvis in a rocking motion, take several deep breaths as you do it then go into slow gentle breathing as your body finds a rhythm. As your hips open, your body can start to tremble naturally, it might be disturbing the first time it happens or it might not happen at all (your brain may not think it's safe) but it can be a good way for your body to process held on to emotions that you may not even be aware of.

January is always the time of year when I just want to hibernate, no matter how enthusiastic I am in my mind, my body just says nope I'm not going anywhere in this weather! Also, I can be happily working away on something on the computer and as soon it gets dark, my mind says well that's it for the day, no more work now!

Now I do not struggle with resting, the more the better, *yes, please*. But it can bring up guilt that I am not doing enough to achieve my intentions or dreams. It can also bring up shame around, this is too easy, I can rest and still live my life/have an income/enjoy myself. This can especially come up if your ancestors were hard workers or had that belief that you must work hard for money.

I know I heard that a lot from my dad, *money doesn't come easy, work isn't easy if you want to have a decent income, you don't get anything for nothing*. I have been clearing a lot of these beliefs that don't belong to me, over the last few years.

Take notice the next time you are resting and hear those thoughts, whose voice is it?

EVEN WHEN WE think we have overcome these beliefs, consciously, we can still have unconscious sabotage. That can manifest in you getting what you have been aiming for and then creating a scenario that puts a stop to it or puts it on hold. Your body is still holding it on a cellular level.

In a new relationship and things are going too well? Time to blame them for something your ex did...

Finally, getting the income you wanted? Go and buy something ridiculous you don't really need because it's hard to hold onto that money.

Got a promotion but don't think you can really do the job even though you have been doing it unofficially? Make a huge mistake that shakes your self-confidence even more.

The key is to go slowly, examine your thoughts, and ask: !s *this mine or somebody else's?*

When I'm less active in the winter, I now think back to hundreds of years ago when my ancestors, who were mostly working the land, would have also been following the patterns of the land, doing less and sleeping more. It's a natural rhythm that electricity and the industrial age made us forget.

Consider what you are eating

The food we eat (or don't eat) can have a big effect on the way we feel. The medical view is that there is no evidence of diet having an effect on our mental state. However, there is lots of anecdotal evidence that it does. It's hard when we are feeling busy or overwhelmed to eat well, a lot of the time we just don't have the energy to cook a proper meal. But when we get home from a long day and we feel hungry we often go for the easiest possible thing, making toast! It satisfies hunger but doesn't give any real energy so your body isn't getting the nutrients it needs. It ends up in a vicious circle, no energy-can't be bothered to cook- make toast- no energy.

I can remember having a conversation with a physiotherapist about diet, he really believed in how it can affect your body but he did tell me that most consultants were cynical about it. He said, *"talking about diet doesn't sell medicine"*. At the time I was having a lot of problems with my knee swelling but there was no evidence of damage to my knee. He suggested that I keep a food diary for a week with the times I had pain or swelling noted down as well. The following week we looked at what I had written and he noticed I ate a lot of yoghurt. I had become particularly fond of those 'fruit corner' yoghurts, I didn't even realise how much I ate them! My task for the next week was to leave them out of my diet and note the effects along with keeping a food diary. I couldn't believe that after 3 days I had no swelling for the rest of the week. It became apparent that the yoghurt seemed related to the joint swelling. Two weeks later I ate yoghurt to test this theory and it did affect my knee.

———

OVER THE YEARS I have refined my diet to what works for me. I am not advising anyone to follow a particular diet but to get to know your body and how it reacts to certain foods. Over the years I have gone through many stages of noting what I eat and how my body reacts. Lots of starchy foods, especially potatoes, make me lethargic. I am now plant-based and try to get in as much fruit and vegetables as I can, although I stay away from anything with high acidic content as I have found this doesn't suit me. You can find out what works for you by doing a food diary for two weeks to see if you can notice any patterns in your energy levels or emotional state.

Drink plenty of water

SOMETIMES YOUR BODY mistakes thirst for hunger and this can cause you to lose focus and sometimes snack when you need a drink. The body is around 70% water so ensuring you are getting in water-based drinks that are not just tea and coffee will help the body and brain feel more alert.

Go to bed at a regular time.

THIS DOES SOUND the most obvious but is often overlooked. Going to bed at a consistent time every night trains your body to know when it's rest time. It's so easy to fall into the trap of only going to bed when you are tired, saying to yourself "If I go to bed now I won't sleep so I will wait until I'm really tired!" or thinking I can catch up on my sleep at the weekend. Even dreading going to bed because it will be another restless night so falling asleep in the armchair. This leads you to wake up in the early hours in your chair or sofa feeling uncomfortable. If you have a partner you get annoyed that they didn't wake you, but they left you there because they didn't want to disturb you so you get some rest! It does take time to establish but going to bed at the same time every night whether you are tired or not gives your body a clear signal that it's sleeping time.

Self-care and self-love are not the same thing

I blame the advertising industry for equating having a massage or going to a spa as self-love. It might make you feel good in the moment but it's not long-term. It's an escape and each time you do something like that as a way to feel better without looking at the root cause it just adds to your anxiety, the feel-good factor goes away sooner each time. It's a distraction from the outside world.

We can also feel guilt around self-care if we saw our parents working hard as a child, especially as a woman and not seeing your Mum take breaks or spend time just for her. We get told that self-care is going for a massage or a beauty treatment when it goes much deeper than that. What if you don't like those things? Self-care is whatever nourishes your soul and brings you back to yourself so you can function around other people in a way that brings you joy. So if you need an hour alone to read, this is self-care. If you want a luxurious bath without someone knocking on the door, this is self-care. It doesn't have to be that one thing you do every week, it can be all those little things throughout the week that add up to you feeling full. The moments that allow you to focus only on yourself, whether that's for 10 minutes or a whole day. When you do them consistently, your body stores these memories and you can access them more frequently during the times when you are busier.

You can spend hundreds of pounds on self-care and still not love yourself. Self-love is a deeper knowing, it's not what you do for yourself it's how you feel about yourself. It's embracing all of you, your faults and your imperfections, your gifts, and your talents for something special. When you fully accept all the parts of you, even the quirky parts. This is self-love.

Self-care can be anything that brings you comfort and joy when you are feeling out of balance.

Have you noticed that you can watch a particular TV series over and over, even though you know what happens? It's your comfort show. It doesn't matter what the storyline is (action or comedy) your mind and body know what is coming next so it does not have to think about it or prepare for a shock. It's especially comforting when you are in a stressful time in your life as you don't need to pay attention to the storyline and the familiarity calms the brain. *My comfort show is Alias.* An action show about black ops spies with Jennifer Garner as the main character, even though there are some dramatic scenes and lots of personal combat it doesn't spike my adrenaline as I know the story so well. I re-watched the whole of season 1 the week after my dad passed away, fully knowing that at the end of every day I could watch a few episodes and completely switch off.

One of the things I do for self-care is to watch an old Hollywood film or Period Drama. It's complete escapism that fills me with joy. Especially Casablanca or Brief Encounter, old-fashioned love stories in black and white, my body is filled with the feel-good factor although both stories are not, particularly the fairytale ending you would want in a love story.

Another thing I like to do to create calm if I am eating lunch on my own, instead of scrolling social media (we've all done it while eating a sandwich) is to listen to an audiobook instead. I love a Jane Austen or historical book for those times, it's soothing to the soul.

Reflections

---

*How much do you give yourself
self-care moments?*

*What can you start doing for
yourself this week?*

CHAPTER 9
CHANGES ARE NOT ALWAYS DELIVERED IN NEAT PACKAGES

There are times in our life when we are so desperate for change but we don't know how to do it or what we want, or we can be implementing small changes but the universe decides that we are not moving fast enough or going in the wrong direction. It can step in with a huge wake-up call or it can play games with you, where you have your hands in the air saying are you kidding me!

Think of the times when you have lost a job or had to move home and it has come about so suddenly, it knocks you off your feet but in the end, it needed to happen for the next thing to come along which was what you wanted or needed. As *A Course in Miracles* says, every relationship is a divine assignment. Those assignments can end abruptly if you have steered off course. When things like this happen I have learned to just go along with it, I keep saying to myself, this is *happening for me, not to me.*

Have you ever had times in your life where you have asked for help from the universe and things have come tumbling down in a way you did not ask for? You ask for a situation to improve but it gets way worse. We don't just have grief when a person dies. Ending a long-standing job and letting go of that old identity and also losing the community you were part of. Losing your physical health and how that impacts your activities. Losing or ending a friendship and the traditions connected to that friendship or community. These can be situations where we are in grief, sometimes without even being aware.

When you ask for help from the divine/God/the universe, be prepared for it to arrive in any shape or form. Also, be prepared for it to arrive in unforeseen circumstances that initially caused you upset or despair. Changes are not always delivered in neat packages with a bow on, but on the other side can lead to the most fortuitous outcomes.

———

SOME YEARS AGO, I had a car accident where the driver drove into the back of my car when I was sitting at red traffic lights. Apart from the damage to my car, which was easily fixed with no cost to me as he admitted full liability, I had whiplash and some rib bruising. Because of the pre-existing condition of my spine condition, this was not included in the insurance claim as the original assessment could not differentiate to what extent the original pain and what consequences were caused by the accident. I was not bothered as my car was fully covered. Roll on 2 years later and I was contacted by the insurance company to have a medical assessment relating to the accident. I thought it was odd as it came out of nowhere. I ended up being given an additional sum (exceeding two thousand pounds) which was the exact extra amount I needed for the life coach training I was about to do so I was able to pay in full. Previous to this, I did not even know where I would get the extra money I needed. I just knew I would get it!

So even though at the time I had extra pain, I had to have time off work and avoided driving down that road for almost two years, preferring to take a longer route so I didn't panic every time I sat at those traffic lights. In the end, it delivered an outcome of exactly what I was asking for.

Of course, there can be terrible times in our lives that we can't see through as having a positive outcome, like death or tragedy. But I feel like when we can connect with something that is greater than ourselves or we can find that peace within regardless of the chaos around us we can know that this too shall pass. When we are faced with unexpected circumstances in our life, it can make us or break us.

————

WHEN MY DAD passed away in 2019 it was life-changing, not just because I was very close to him but I was surprised at people's reaction to how I coped with it. My dad had lung cancer so we knew that he did not have long at the end and because I had spent almost every day there in the last few months it was not a big shock or like it was unexpected. To me it was like he had walked into the next room, I could still talk to him. It was just his physical body not there. I held on to that belief as I had to do all the death admin (oh so much!)and expressed it to a few family members when asked how I was coping. They didn't quite get it and said I was in denial, but I would say if I was in denial I wouldn't be organising a funeral would I. Every day I held onto the belief that the universe is bigger than us, life is transient and we have to continue to live.

People say when a parent dies it's different from any other bereavement you have but you don't quite realise what that means until you live it. I was able to do a special personal goodbye to him and it brought peace to me in every moment. I took some of his ashes to every place he lived and loved around the country. Even the betting shops and snooker halls he went to, that was quite comical as you can imagine I had to go there at 6.30 am on a Sunday so no one would see me scatter ashes outside! I had one final journey with him with my cousin on the first day of our second lockdown in 2020. It was a lovely sunny day and our last trip was to a golf course he loved. My initial plan had been to scatter him outside the clubhouse, but as the course was shut we managed to get him on the tee of the first hole! Now he can haunt people forever when they don't play a good shot. It was a lovely ceremonial ending to mark his life.

———

SOMETIMES WE CAN ASK the universe for guidance and support and be given it in the most profound way. I went to a little-known druid site in Kent with a friend, an old burial mound that still has some of the stones on top all laid out in part of a circle. We sat on one of the stones and meditated, asking for guidance and support from our ancestors. My friend went to lay an offering of flowers at the altar and as I stood up I saw a feather on the ground behind the stones. I went to pick it up, lost my footing and there was a great gust of wind from nowhere that knocked me off my feet.

It all happened as if it was slow motion

I fell forwards towards the edge of the mound. It's about 20 feet high, and I got close to the edge, my head just about to fall in the bush growing up the side, I was pushed backward, stumbled back onto a stone, plonked down, and then lay down on my back. It was as if someone or something had stopped me from falling over the edge and laid me down on the stone. I lay there for a moment stunned, assessing whether I had hurt anything in the fall.

My friend rushed over asking if I was ok and I said "wow that felt like it was slow motion" it was a bit scary, and she said, "no it was slow motion". I had gone down with a thud on the stone and was expecting not to be able to get up or walk, but although I was sore I was all right. If I had fallen over the edge I'm not sure I would have come out of that walking. *To me it was saying, you want to change?* OK then how about this to shake you up a bit? When we went back to my friend's house we did a gratitude ceremony, being grateful for everything in our lives around the fire and burning what we no longer needed.

Here is a simple ceremony you can do for gratitude...

MARK 3 COLUMNS ON PAPER. In the first column, write everything you are grateful for that has brought you to the current moment but you no longer need. In the second column, write things you are grateful for and that you would like to keep. In the third column, write things that you are grateful for and would like more of and things that you would like to welcome into your life.

You can do this in a gratitude journal if you have one, or like me can just use a piece of paper and burn it after. Always burn safely outside. If like me you live in apartments, you can use a cup or bowl to burn it outside. Then throw the ashes to the wind. In a previous place I lived, I would stand outside just feet away from the public path burning stuff in a cup, and even though the odd passer-by looked confused no one ever said anything to me, not even my neighbours!

There are so many times in my life where I have had life-changing situations forced on me by external circumstances: being made redundant; having to move home because the landlord was selling the property; having to give up work because of ill health. Years later I could see that each one of these has led me to make choices I probably would not have been presented with. It's like the eternal sliding doors moments—one thing has led to another which has brought me to today.

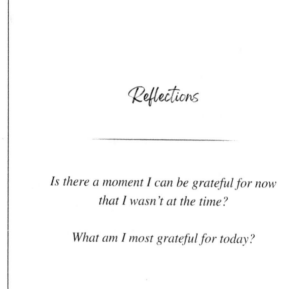

Reflections

---

*Is there a moment I can be grateful for now
that I wasn't at the time?*

What am I most grateful for today?

CHAPTER 10
WRONG MOTIVATION OR PROCRASTINATION?

Have you ever thought you are a big procrastinator?

That might not be the case, it could be that you don't know where your motivation comes from.

Some people have intrinsic motivation, which means we have great self-control when it comes to deadlines, we can self-reward for completing tasks and we don't need anyone to remind us, we also usually complete things before the deadline.

If you are someone that needs extrinsic motivation, you will not respond to self-set deadlines and won't rush to finish anything unless someone else is pressing you for a result. And you respond greatly to someone encouraging you along the way. Often, we don't know we are motivated by extrinsic rewards or motivation, so we call ourselves procrastinators or wonder why something is so hard to achieve. I did two whole degrees this way, doing every assignment in the last 2 to 3 weeks of a semester! Even though every term I would say at the 3-month mark when we got the assignment, "ok this time I will set it out like this with the planning of each section, if I finish that part by this date, then I can have time to write section by section" every single time I just skipped to I'll start next week, down to getting to 3 weeks away and saying oh f*ck better start now!

I now realise it's because I need someone else to enforce deadlines and hold me to account, otherwise I'm so chilled I won't do it without realising the urgency of a task. What I needed was the tutor checking in and seeing how far I had gotten, but it was adult education so they think you are self-responsible.

This is also the reason long to-do lists don't work for me, it needs to be three things max on a list. If there are more than three things to do when organising, I take the three *most important things* (abbreviated to my MITs) that need to be done first, then move them onto a separate list.

———

THE OTHER THING that creates what we think is procrastination is perfection. Not wanting to start something until the right moment because not everything is in place or doing irrelevant things that won't make any difference to the outcome but in our minds, these are important to get done before starting the actual task. For example, choosing the 'right font' before sitting down to write and then giving up because you are overwhelmed with choice. Getting overwhelmed by the image of the fantasy outcome (which is often some perfect almost impossible scenario) so not taking the first step because it won't turn out as good as that. Having to know what the whole thing will look like in a joint project even though the other part is not your specialty, but not trusting that the other person knows what it is they need to do. This can result in over-checking every step even though you don't understand it. This holds up the starting of the project and causes frustration and can even end up in it not happening at all because the other person loses patience and breaks away.

So what about you?

Is your motivation intrinsic or extrinsic, or do you recognise yourself as a perfectionist? It can be really helpful when you realise it.

I do think routines can be helpful in getting over low motivation and how you start your day is a big one.

I love my morning routine

AND AS YOU know I will not tell you to get up at 5 am (unless of course, you are getting on a plane). How you start your day is important and it doesn't have to be some long-drawn-out ritual, mine can take anywhere between thirty minutes to one hour depending on what my day looks like and if I have to go out early. The easiest thing to implement that will have a big impact on your cortisol levels in the morning when you wake up is not reaching for your phone immediately or putting on the TV.

If you use your phone as your alarm, my tip is to use a normal alarm clock, or use an old phone just for the alarm, and put your actual phone out of reach of your bed. This stops you from automatically reaching out for your phone when you wake up in the morning, or even in the middle of the night.

Before I go to sleep I turn off the sound on my phone along with the mobile data and the WiFi connection, and if I am at home I turn it off completely. When I get up and I am waiting for the kettle to boil (after the bathroom obviously) it means that when I turn on my phone I don't see any emails or messages pop up. Even with your notifications off, they will still pop up at the top, you don't need this first thing. While I'm drinking my tea I listen to an affirmations audio, so my adrenaline is not spiked by hearing or seeing other people's requests or news. As I mentioned before, our body produces cortisol during sleep for repair, which can stay in our body for up to thirteen hours in the day, so we need that first twenty to thirty minutes in the morning to start the day producing oxytocin.

If I am sitting having a drink anyway, why not listen to something empowering instead of doom scrolling or hearing bad news. Then I'll meditate for 5 or 10 minutes, just focusing on the in and out breaths. I use a timer, say a quick prayer to the angels and my guides and that's it.

On days when I have more time before an appointment or something I need to do, I will write in my book about an ideal day, but I write it from the future as if it already happened. It's another way to flood your body with oxytocin. You might like to add in a walk or some sort of exercise, whatever gives you the feel-good chemicals.

I don't turn on my data or Wi-Fi until I have been up for forty-five minutes to an hour, so I have created a buffer zone for anything coming my way. It sets up my day feeling calm and positive and ready to face the outside world.

There are so many tools we can use to create calm and balance in our everyday life but not all tools fit all people. I love to meditate but I know friends who just can't do it. When I say meditate, I mean sitting in silence and focusing on my breathe or doing a visualisation. But meditation to you might be a moving meditation such as dance, walking, or cycling. It is whatever connects us to our joy or purpose and lets us tune into our higher self or get those messages from God or spirit.

Many of us don't meditate because we think we can't, *"I can't stop the thoughts"* people will say to me and my reply is, *"good you're not meant to"*. It's about being aware of our thoughts, not stopping them. When you notice you are having random thoughts about yesterday, tomorrow, or ten years ago, you say to yourself 'oh I'm thinking, come back to the moment' and you return to your breath or your focus. At some point, you will notice that the gaps between the thoughts are longer, and you can maintain your focus more and more. But in today's modern world we are never going to stop our thoughts, we don't live in caves in the middle of nowhere with no responsibilities.

Time management is another thing that can create calm and balance

WE OFTEN UNDERESTIMATE how long things will take to do or travel to. Time is a man-made construct that we all have to fit into at some point in our life. As much as you might want to not be controlled by time if you have an appointment at 2 pm you need to be there by 2 pm!

It can be easy for time to escape you when you are doing something enjoyable, we always say the time went so fast, or the time just dragged when it's something we don't like doing. But what if you are one of those people that just can't seem to be on time anywhere? Or do you never have enough time? You need to be realistic about how much you can do in a day, it really is that simple. If you find yourself making commitments and then having to cancel because you ran out of time, then you need to ask yourself are you overcommitting and saying yes when you want to say no, or are you forgetting to factor in everyday tasks like eating, dressing and traveling?

When was I learning how to manage fatigue, I learned about The Spoon Theory, it has helped over the years explain to others the difference between being tired and having fatigue. It says that we have a limited number of spoons to use each day, ten for example, and we can't carry them over to the next day. If it takes three spoons to have a shower and wash your hair, then you have seven spoons left for the day so we need to think carefully about how we spend them. Two spoons to prepare breakfast and one to make an important phone call, then you have four left, you might not want to use them doing something unnecessary because you still have to get through the day.

It might not be like this every day but it can be helpful for assessing your own energy when you are not feeling great and also it can be much easier to say to a friend, I'm sorry I don't have enough spoons to do that right now, without having to go into a long explanation if you don't want to.

Are you using all of your time in the most productive way for you?

THIS DOESN'T MEAN CRAMMING every hour with getting things done and always having to achieve something, but are there things that you waste more time on without even realising? Do you find yourself getting a breather with a cup of tea thinking *"yes I've got ten minutes to relax"* but then you pick up your phone scroll, social media, and are not relaxed at all?

When that happens try one of these instead:

STAND OUTSIDE (without your phone) and just breathe, or tend to some plants. If you have some flowers do a quick survey for any dead flowers that need to be pinched out. If you are unable to go outside look out of a window.

Make a ten-minute playlist with three songs that make you feel good.

Do some colouring in

Read or listen to 1 chapter of a book

Being more mindful in those ten minutes will make a bigger impact on your mind and body and you will feel more relaxed than you did from ten minutes of doom scrolling with no purpose.

Reflections

How am I motivated for personal tasks?

*Can I optimise my morning routine
for a better start to the day?*

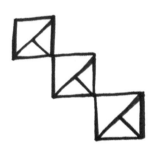

CHAPTER 11
WHAT BRINGS YOU JOY?

D o you have interests that are solely for you that bring you joy? Or do you have a hobby that you can share with others? When we make time for ourselves by doing something fulfilling, that fills our cups so we can then feel full enough to give to others. When we spend all our leisure or personal time doing things without a real interest, maybe because it's a friend or partner's hobby or because it's expected of us we can become bored, resentful, and tired. Doing things for ourselves is not selfish it's self full, we feel more satisfied with our life so we joyfully give to and help others.

Turn off the news. It will just spike your adrenaline or make you angry. I haven't watched the news for a long time and am still aware of what is happening in the world. It doesn't matter where you are in the world, most TV news is a form of propaganda, with its own slant to the story depending on their political leaning, most of the time they are not sharing news, they are sharing an opinion. It can drive you to despair and think the world is a fearful place, with its wall-to-wall coverage of the terrible things in the world. I remember the news back in the '70s, it was on twice a day and the evening news normally ended with some quirky item or funny incident. Before the 24-hour news cycle became big business we usually got one or two sides of the story, and we got along just fine. I don't ignore what is happening but I don't need to hear the same thing repeated several times a day. This will not bring you joy.

I believe that when we have a moment of joy every day it keeps our cup of calm flowing over. It doesn't have to be something big every day either. If it brings you laughter or makes you smile that is enough. It could be something you hadn't even considered before that activates your calm like playing with a pet, or singing out loud even though you can't sing, be present with it and see the difference it makes to your joy levels.

For a quick boost of laughter, I will go and watch a Joe Lycett video on YouTube. There is something about the line 'hopefully doth butter no parsnips' in my personal favorite that makes me laugh so much every time. You can actually Google his name with that line and get the video. It's that well searched for!

As I have gotten older I have engaged more in a real love of history, especially Tudor times and the Regency era. In my younger years, I would not have been so open about it in case people think I am boring but I have been told that I have a good memory for the facts of those times so have given myself permission to be a full-on geek about it. When I used to skip school at fifteen and sixteen, I used to go into central London and look at the buildings and wander around places like The National Gallery and the Natural History Museum. I often would say I got a better education that way than I did at school. I was never questioned about why I was there alone. I think the staff just assumed I was on a school trip and had wandered off. At least it was better than hanging around the park like the other truants.

When we uphold our personal values we honour ourselves. What if we don't really know what our values are or have just made the assumption that we know. Sure, we can say our values are being kind to others, having a good work ethic, and being honest. But are they just the values that we were instilled with growing up? And what if we have witnessed a contradiction in values from our parents and other adults, you have to work hard to get anywhere but also it's ok to cheat to get ahead if it doesn't really hurt anyone. Be kind to others but if someone hits you hit back. Be honest but sometimes it's ok to tell a white lie.

This can create an internal moral dilemma between what we feel is right and what we see in action.

Do any kind of values exercise (it's standard at lots of personal development events) and we normally say what we think we value or what we want more of and we only get ten minutes to write them down. I used to say freedom was one of my values but when I spent some time really thinking about them it's not that high on the list. My top values are connection, community, and trust, followed by joy and adventure. I value personal relationships over the freedom to travel. You will know when one of your values is not being respected as you will likely feel shut down or out of place. Every time I have started to feel like I was not enjoying being at a place of work, I can now see it was because my top values were not being honored. When I have worked in schools where we felt like a team and all the staff got along and was able to communicate with each other well, fostering a sense of community and trust with each other it has been a joy to be at work. When that changes, either through a change of management or certain staff leaving it changes the way people relate to each other. It not only affects your relationships with each other but also your environment.

I think that our environment has a massive effect on

how we activate our calm both at home and at work. Wherever we spend a great amount of time will have an impact on our mental state and physical self.

Does your environment express who you are?

I AM a fan of decluttering and being tidy but I am not a fan of the extreme approach of Mari Kondo, I mean, who only has six books or less in their home! And yes there is something in keeping things that bring you joy but it can go too far with the minimalist lifestyle, we all need to feel like we belong somewhere and not in a show home. Our everyday environment needs to make us feel connected to ourselves in a way that brings comfort and ease, we are not robots designed to live in blank rooms with white walls.

Ever noticed that it's much easier to work on a tidy desk? Sounds obvious right but then some people have piles of paper everywhere and still seem to get things done. Being surrounded by piles of paper or unfinished tasks is not giving your brain the optimum environment to get things done. There will be some low-level anxiety or distraction around the other things that need to be done, this can often lead to procrastination. As I have said before we don't multitask, we multi-focus. As I have been writing this book I have had to make sure I have done the laundry the day before so as not to be distracted by it or use it as a reason not to write! Just a quick tidy of the immediate environment before either starting work or an important task at home will create more focus. And creating a home or space at work that feels personal and reflects part of our personality, even in the smallest way can give us a feeling of comfort.

Are you holding onto things from the past, not for sentimental reasons but just in case? When we can't let go of things it can be because we are scared of moving forward, of not knowing what is next. We can hold onto old clothes that no longer fit as a way of holding on to that version of ourselves. Hoarding can be a way of saying, I don't feel safe, I need a barrier around me. We can hold onto the most irrelevant things just in case with no logic and it can be hard to ask ourselves 'why do I need this?'

On occasions when I have decluttered and organised homes for people, it's so interesting to see what people hold onto and why. I remember finding a folder of floppy disks in a drawer, years after they could be actually used in a computer or converted in any way. This person said they had important information. When I asked them 'how would you get this information if you needed it?' they didn't know so it went in the bin. Of course, they panicked and also tried to get it out while I was in the bathroom. Sometimes our brain tells us 'But you need that it's important way after it's any use to us.

I know I have mentioned sleep a few times and how important it is but it's always something I hone in on when someone says they are always tired. *Your sleeping habits and routine have a huge role in your daily calm.* Anxiety and discomfort can cause us to wake up repeatedly during the night causing sleep disturbance, then we don't get the deep sleep needed to refresh our body so we can wake up from a night's sleep feeling exhausted.

When you are not going into a deep sleep you are easily disturbed by events in the environment such as light and noise. I found sleep disturbance one of the hardest things to deal with when waking up four or five times during the night at the worst part of my chronic illness. There are a number of things you can do to ensure your sleeping environment supports you in getting a good night's sleep.

Unless you are living in a house-share or bedsit, remove the TV from the bedroom. If you have no choice about having the TV in the room where you sleep, don't put it on at bedtime. I know that it seems like watching TV to fall asleep will help you but it creates blue light and noise pollution that will disturb you later on in the night. Even watching television in bed with the intention of turning it off before sleep, sends the wrong signals to your conscious mind. Your mental state will be heightened and not in the calm state you need to promote good sleep.

You need to send a clear message to your brain that the bed is for sleeping. If you are living in a shared home and cannot remove your TV make a point of sitting in a different place to watch it so your bed is not associated with it. Or make sure you sit up on the bed for watching TV and lay down for sleeping. You can also cover it with a cloth when it's not being used this will really create intentional watching and enforce the idea that the bed is for resting.

Make sure your hands and feet are warm so you can be comfortable. Consider the weight of the bedclothes, if you have a duvet that's not warm enough, think about getting a higher tog rating instead of adding blankets on top, they might seem light in theory but can sometimes feel oppressive. Poor circulation can often be associated with high anxiety conditions so even in the summer you should make sure you have appropriate cover for sleeping to maintain a good body temperature. Make sure you are not disturbed by light pollution during the night from street lights, car headlights, and the rising sun by having appropriate window coverings. These can easily wake you in a light sleep cycle, and with the light, it can be harder to get back to sleep.

Another thing that can help us feel calmer in our environment is interacting with nature.

This does not mean you have to go on a hike in the woods every week. We can easily bring nature into our homes, having a plant is not only good for the actual environment of your home, (breathing in our carbon dioxide and breathing out oxygen for us) tending to plants encourages mindfulness. It can also create serotonin (the feel-good hormone) in us by having something to nurture and interact with. And yes I do chat to my plants, I say when I give them water, I apologise if I need to remove a dying leaf and I say well done when growing a new bud. Even if you believe you are no good with plants and forget to water them, just one small one in a bathroom or kitchen where there is access to water when you remember will help.

Do you have space to grow food? Even a windowsill for a pot of herbs to add to your food. This helps us immensely with the feel-good factor of chemicals and positive reinforcement of doing something for yourself.

Reflections

Am I happy with my environment?

Is there something I can do differently?

CALM IS WITHIN YOU

As you have gone through this book, I hope you have come to see that calm, like love, is within you.

We can be in the most chaotic place or situation and still access our calm if we know how to connect with it.

I hope that you have learned that we can all access our calm, and still live our lives. It's not about being zen every moment of the day. When you are aware of your feelings you can come into the moment and activate your calm as long as you need to. We are human beings, and we all ride a rollercoaster of emotions every day, unless, of course, you are sitting in a room not seeing anyone or doing anything, you will need to navigate your own feelings and other people's. Tune into the inner satnav (GPS) and listen to the guidance, your voice will lead you the way.

———

Here is a list of my favorite resources for creating Calm and things I have referred to in the book

You can get my free resource on understanding EFT in my free Calm Up Kit on my website samlivermore.com this includes a how-to video along with a chart for the tapping points. Along with my daily affirmations audio and a few other helpful resources for Calm.

At Zero by Joe Vitale - a book about the ho'pono'pono and how he came across it.

Online Video '**Water, Consciousness and Intent**' Dr. Masaru Emoto

Insight Timer App - a free app for meditation, I like to use the timer on there for when I do silent focus on the breath. You can set it as a singing bowl or chimes.

The Alchemist by Paulo Coelho, is recommended by so many people and he is my favorite author so had to include this if you have not read it. However, my favorite book of his is Veronika Decides to Die, which follows the story of a young woman who takes an overdose and wakes up in a psychiatric ward. It is a wonderful life-affirming story.

The Tip Off by Elizabeth Peru. Elizabeth Peru looks at the energetic flow of the planets and how it affects the earth and ourselves, it's more than just astrology its about being in harmony with nature. Her daily forecasts really help me understand how to work with my personal energy.

This is Mozart playlist online. This whole book has been written while listening to it.

The Spoon Theory - butyoudontlooksick.com/category/the-spoon-theory/

Being around moving water. Whether it's the waves of the seashore breaking on the beach or the flow of a stream, there is something both cleansing and calming in watching the water. See my highlights reel on Instagram called Calming Waves.

Joe Lycett. Hopefully doth butter no parsnips
   youtube.com/watch?v=2Gkiw7zpULo

And finally, of course, *writing a letter to a stranger.* Sometimes those words to a stranger are what you need to hear and it can bring you back to yourself.
   See my first book *100 Letters to A Stranger*

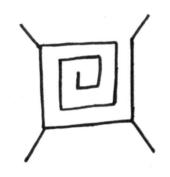

ACKNOWLEDGMENTS

Thank you to my publishers Sean and Karen. Sean for your friendship and for giving me the phrase Calm Up several years ago when trying to describe to me what I did. Karen for your mentorship and prayers as I wrote this book.

My friends who have been on this ride with me, supporting me whether they know it or not. Elyse, Kelley, and Leila you have all said things to keep me going while I was writing.

My parents and grandparents who have given me the wisdom to be who I am today and my ancestors before that.

JOIN THE MOVEMENT

WWW.SHARETHELOVELETTERS.COM

ABOUT THE AUTHOR

Sam Livermore was born in London. She trained as a psychodynamic counsellor completing her training in 2001 and went on to work in education for 14 years. She is a Personal Performance Life Coach, Reiki Master Teacher, EFT Practitioner, and Crystal therapist. She combines all of this in her mixed modality approach with her Calm Up sessions.

She is the founder of sharetheloveletters.com and author of 100 Letters to A Stranger. You can find her leaving love letters around events and places of interest.

She grew up in Edmonton and once played the spoons with Chas and Dave (that great cockney duo). She has great musical timing but a shocking singing voice. Every one of her school reports said if she put as much into her work as she did talking she would be more successful in her efforts.

facebook.com/samgladiatoroflove
instagram.com/sam_gladiator_of_love

CPSIA information can be obtained
at www.ICGtesting.com
Printed in the USA
LVHW012206031022
729859LV00014B/516